MOOSE

By Rachel Rose

Minneapolis, Minnesota

Credits
Cover and title page, © Harry Collins/iStock; 3, © MuhammadAsif6/Shutterstock; 4–5, © georgesanker.com/Alamy Stock Photo; 6, © Wirestock Creators/Shutterstock; 7, © Colleen Gara/Getty Images; 9, © FerBozaPhoto/Shutterstock; 10–11, © Mc Photo/Alamy Stock Photo; 13, © Dennis Stogsdill/Shutterstock; 14, © Freder/iStock; 15, © Eastcott Momatiuk/iStock; 16, © wanderluster/iStock; 17, © Matthew/Adobe Stock; 18–19, © Design Pics Inc/Alamy Stock Photo; 21, © Leola Durant/iStock; 22L, © msan10/iStock; 22R, © johnnylemonseed/iStock; 23, © Design Pics Inc/Alamy Stock Photo.

Bearport Publishing Company Product Development Team
Publisher: Jen Jenson; Director of Product Development: Spencer Brinker; Managing Editor: Allison Juda; Editor: Cole Nelson; Associate Editor: Naomi Reich; Associate Editor: Tiana Tran; Designer: Kim Jones; Designer: Kayla Eggert; Designer: Steve Scheluchin; Production Specialist: Owen Hamlin

Statement on Usage of Generative Artificial Intelligence
Bearport Publishing remains committed to publishing high-quality nonfiction books. Therefore, we restrict the use of generative AI to ensure accuracy of all text and visual components pertaining to a book's subject. See BearportPublishing.com for details.

Library of Congress Cataloging-in-Publication Data is available at www.loc.gov or upon request from the publisher.

ISBN: 979-8-89577-046-7 (hardcover)
ISBN: 979-8-89577-470-0 (paperback)
ISBN: 979-8-89577-163-1 (ebook)

Copyright © 2026 Bearport Publishing Company. All rights reserved. No part of this publication may be reproduced in whole or in part, stored in any retrieval system, or transmitted in any form or by any means, electronic, mechanical, photocopying, recording, or otherwise, without written permission from the publisher. Bearport Publishing is a division of FlutterBee Education Group.

For more information, write to Bearport Publishing, 5357 Penn Avenue South, Minneapolis, MN 55419.

Contents

Awesome Moose! 4
Meet the Moose 6
Wintry Homes 8
Water Lovers 10
Hungry Herbivores 12
Amazing Antlers 14
Danger, Deer! 16
Fight for Love 18
Young Moose 20

Information Station 22
Glossary 23
Index 24
Read More 24
Learn More Online 24
About the Author 24

AWESOME Moose!

SNAP! Reaching up, the moose bites some twigs off a tree's branches. The towering creature chomps down, making a quick meal of the woody treat. Big and strong, moose are awesome!

MOOSE ARE SOME OF THE TALLEST **MAMMALS** IN NORTH AMERICA.

Meet the Moose

Moose are the largest **species** of deer. A **male** moose can weigh up to 1,600 pounds (700 kg). That's heavier than a grand piano! To hold up their large bodies, the animals have long, strong legs with hooves on the bottom of their feet. These wide hooves act as snowshoes, helping heavy moose walk on top of snow without sinking.

MOOSE HAVE A FLAP OF SKIN UNDER THEIR CHIN CALLED A DEWLAP (DOO-LAP).

Wintry Homes

There are eight **subspecies** of moose found around the world. They live mostly in the northern forests of Europe, Russia, and North America. Moose are often found in mountain areas that have cold, snowy winters. **BRR!** They spend a lot of time in bodies of water, including rivers, lakes, and ponds.

> THE LARGEST MOOSE POPULATION IS IN CANADA. THE COUNTRY IS HOME TO AS MANY AS 1 MILLION OF THEM!

Water Lovers

On warm summer days, moose head to the water to keep cool. **SPLASH!** Despite their large size, moose are fast swimmers. They can swim up to 6 miles per hour (10 kph). What else makes moose great in the water? They can float thanks to their two coats of fur. The top layer of fur is made of hollow hairs that keep them up in water.

MOOSE CAN STAY UNDERWATER FOR UP TO 30 SECONDS AT A TIME.

Hungry Herbivores

Moose are **herbivores**. They eat mostly twigs and the bark of trees in the winter. When there is more food in the spring and summer, the animals munch on leaves, fruit, and water plants. **YUM!** These huge creatures can eat up to 70 lbs. (30 kg) of food a day. It can take them hours of chowing down to fill up their large stomachs.

MOOSE HAVE THICK LIPS AND TONGUES THAT HELP THEM EAT WOODY MEALS.

Amazing Antlers

While moose are best known for their huge antlers, only the males have the fancy headgear. One pair of antlers can weigh up to 50 lbs. (22 kg). That's about as heavy as a medium-sized dog! Most male moose **shed** their antlers before winter and grow new ones in the spring. It can take a few months for antlers to fully grow to their large size.

AS THEY ARE GROWING, ANTLERS ARE COVERED IN SHORT, SOFT FUR CALLED VELVET.

Danger, Deer!

Black bears and grizzly bears are very dangerous to moose. While bears often hunt baby moose, they can easily kill adults, too. Wolves and humans who hunt moose for meat are also a **threat** to these big deer.

A grizzly bear

Fight for Love

Moose are mostly **solitary** creatures. This changes during **mating season** in late September. A **female** moose usually picks her mate based on the size and strength of his antlers. But if two males want the same mate, they will fight one another. The female chooses the winner. After about eight months, she will give birth to one or two babies, called calves.

A MALE MOOSE IS CALLED A BULL, AND A FEMALE IS A COW.

Young Moose

Young calves stick close to their mothers. The little moose grow quickly and can run after only about five days. They will stay in their mother's care for almost a year. Then, when she is ready to give birth to a new baby, the young moose leave to live life on their own until they're around four or five. At that time, they are old enough to mate and have young.

> MOOSE CAN LIVE FOR ABOUT 12 YEARS IN THE WILD.

Information Station

MOOSE ARE AWESOME!
LET'S LEARN MORE ABOUT THEM.

Kind of animal: Moose are mammals. Most mammals have fur, give birth to live young, and drink milk from their mothers as babies.

Size: Moose can grow up to 6.5 feet (2 m), from hoof to shoulder. That's taller than most adult men.

Other deer: There are more than 40 different species of deer. The white-tailed deer is the most common, with about 35 million found around the world.

MOOSE AROUND THE WORLD

Arctic Ocean
NORTH AMERICA
EUROPE
ASIA
Pacific Ocean
Atlantic Ocean
AFRICA
Indian Ocean
Pacific Ocean
SOUTH AMERICA
AUSTRALIA
Southern Ocean
ANTARCTICA

Where Moose Live

22

Glossary

dewlap a fold of loose skin that hangs from the neck of an animal

female a moose that can give birth to young

herbivores animals that eat only plants

male a moose that cannot give birth to young

mammals animals that have hair or fur, give birth to live young, and drink milk from their mothers as babies

mating season the time of year when animals come together to have young

shed to lose antlers

solitary living alone

species groups that animals are divided into, according to similar characteristics

subspecies a small category of animals that are similar but not quite the same

threat someone or something that might cause harm

Index

antlers 14, 16, 18
calves 18, 20
dewlap 6
female 18–19
fur 10, 14, 22
herbivores 12
hooves 6, 16
male 6, 14, 18–19
mating 18
plants 12
species 6, 22
threat 16
water 8, 10, 12

Read More

Hubbard, Ben. *Wolves vs. Moose: Food Chain Fights (Predator vs. Prey).* Minneapolis: Lerner Publications, 2025.

Mason, Jenny. *Moose (North American Wildlife).* Minneapolis: Kaleidoscope, 2023.

Learn More Online

1. Go to **FactSurfer.com** or scan the QR code below.
2. Enter "**Moose**" into the search box.
3. Click on the cover of this book to see a list of websites.

About the Author

Rachel Rose writes books for kids and teaches yoga. Her favorite animal of all is her dog, Sandy.